Incredible Underground Homes

Written by Mary-Anne Creasy

Flying Start
to Literacy®

Contents

Introduction

For thousands of years people have lived in homes under the ground. Living underground protected them from the weather and helped them hide from their enemies. The earliest types of underground homes were often caves. Sometimes whole communities lived together underground.

Living underground is not just something that happened a long time ago. Today, some people choose to live in underground homes. Many of these people live in natural caves. Other people have excavated enormous houses underground that are very comfortable and spacious.

Living underground protects people from very hot and very cold weather. As it does not get too hot or cold, underground homes do not need to be heated or cooled. This saves energy and is good for the environment. Building homes under the ground could be the way of the future.

These rock dwellings in Turkey are thousands of years old.

Chapter 1
An underground city

There is a place in Turkey where a whole city was once built underground. The city had hundreds of rooms, and tunnels that connected them.

Today, modern houses are built in among the ancient homes in Cappadocia, in Turkey.

The first homes in this city were excavated thousands of years ago. People used basic tools made from metal and stone to dig into the ground. The digging wasn't too hard because the ground was made of volcanic rock, which is a soft rock. Eventually these homes became part of a huge underground city.

The underground city was built by the people to protect them from the weather. In this area, the winters are freezing and the summers are very hot. Under the ground the temperature is not too hot or cold, and it almost always stays the same. By living underground the people were insulated from the cold and heat.

The underground city also helped to protect the people from their enemies. Some archaeologists believe that these people were often attacked. When this happened, they hid in their underground city. Sometimes they needed to hide for months and were forced to take everything they needed to survive underground.

They needed to store and cook food so they made kitchens and chimneys to let out smoke from cooking fires. They needed water so they dug wells.

Incredible underground fact

Archaeologists have discovered 10 levels of caves at Cappadocia going down 85 metres. They believe up to 50 000 people could have lived there.

This room was carved from rock under the ground in Cappadocia.

They had to bring their farm animals, so they dug out stables. They even dug out rooms to make schools for the children.

The people needed air and light when they were underground so they dug long, narrow shafts up to the surface. The shafts let in light and air but kept out rain and wind.

They also made shafts so that people on different levels could talk to each other.

Chapter 2
Cave houses

In Matmata, Tunisia, an underground village was built around a huge pit in the ground. The village was made by digging deep into the ground to make the pit. This pit became the central courtyard for the village. Rooms, stairways and passages were then excavated from inside the pit. These rooms became cave houses for the people to live in.

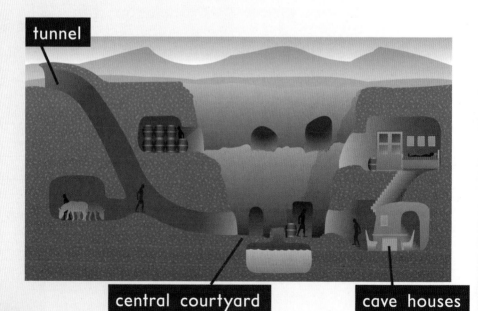

tunnel

central courtyard

cave houses

The central courtyard for the village in Matmata, today.

This room is under the ground in Matmata.

By living underground, the people were protected from the harsh, dry climate. The underground village was also a great hiding place from enemies. The only way in and out was through a tunnel that led to the surface.

Incredible underground Fact

The underground village in Matmata was so well hidden in the desert that the rest of the world did not know it existed until about 40 years ago.

Archaeologists think the village is about 1000 years old, but they are not certain. Over the years, long periods of rain have caused many of these underground homes to collapse. The houses have been repaired many times, which makes it hard to see exactly how old they are.

Visitors can look inside the houses and even stay in an underground hotel.

Chapter 3

Built into cliffs

Some people have made their homes in the sides of mountains underneath cliffs. These cliffs have provided shelter for many communities around the world.

Mesa Verde National Park

In the Mesa Verde National Park in Colorado, USA, there are huge sandstone cliffs. Over 900 years ago Native Americans lived underneath these cliffs. The space beneath the overhanging cliffs is so big that it forms a huge, shallow cave. This cave protected the Native Americans from the harsh weather.

The Native Americans built their homes under the cliffs using sandstone blocks. They joined the blocks together using a mixture of soil, water and ash. Some of the buildings had more than 100 rooms where nearly 200 people could have lived.

Archaeologists think that people lived in this cliff village for about 100 years. The people then suddenly left, but archaeologists cannot figure out why.

Today, people can still see parts of this cliff village.

La Roque Saint Christophe

In the south-west of France there is a network of caves in a cliff made out of limestone. Limestone is a soft rock so people were able to carve out large shelters using very basic stone tools. People lived in these cave shelters a long, long time ago, before history was recorded. These are known as prehistoric times.

Thousands of years later people built houses in the caves. The houses were high up on a cliff. The people were able to see their enemies coming and could protect themselves.

People entered their homes by climbing ladders. The ladders were then pulled up so that their enemies could not get into their homes. People lived in the cliff-side village for 1000 years. They left the village when they no longer had enemies they needed protection from.

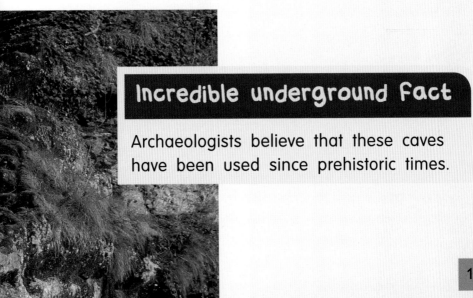

Incredible underground fact

Archaeologists believe that these caves have been used since prehistoric times.

Chapter 4

Living underground today

Spanish cave houses

Today, thousands of people live in cave houses in southern Spain. It is a very dry, hot place. In summer the temperature reaches 40.5 degrees Celsius. Underground it is about 21 degrees Celsius all year. It is much more comfortable for people to live underground.

Cave houses were originally carved by hand into the side of hills and cliffs. Today houses are excavated using modern machinery.

Incredible underground fact

Historians think that Arabs brought the idea of living underground to southern Spain more than 1000 years ago.

These cave houses are in Granada
in southern Spain.

From the outside these houses look tiny
but inside they are roomy and comfortable.
Stone chimneys provide fresh air to the
homes and light comes through holes made
by huge drills.

A town under the desert

In the Australian desert there is an underground town called Coober Pedy. Precious stones called opals are mined there. People live underground in Coober Pedy to escape the extreme heat. Their houses are made by digging deep into the sandstone ground. Sandstone is not too hard to dig, and it's stable and strong, which helps to make the houses safe.

From outside an underground house in Coober Pedy, all that can be seen is a door in the side of a hill and a pipe sticking out of the ground. These pipes are the ventilation shafts that let in air. Inside the houses, the walls and ceilings are coated with clear paint to prevent dust. Some of the houses are mansions with gyms and swimming pools.

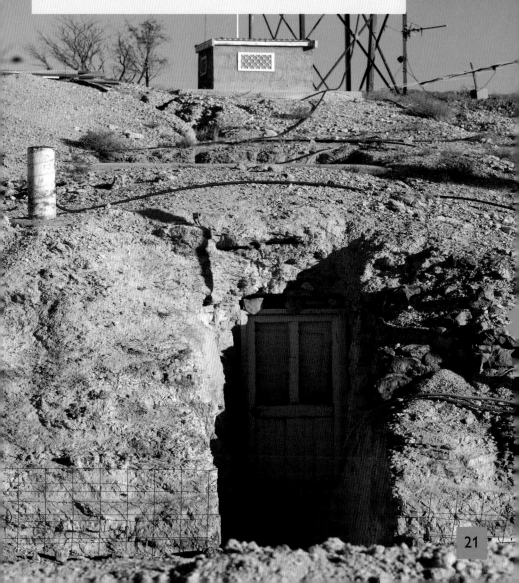

Incredible underground fact

The temperature in summer can reach more than 48 degrees Celsius during the day – it gets so hot that people play golf at night!

Chapter 5

Blending in

Today, many underground houses blend into the places where they are built. These houses are almost invisible from a distance, but inside they can be huge  mansions with enormous, light-filled rooms.

To build a modern underground house, tonnes of earth and rock are removed by heavy machinery. When the house is built, the rock and earth are pushed back around and on top of the house.

Windows in the roof or on the side let in light. And they have shafts that let in light and air, just as they did thousands of years ago in Turkey.

This enormous modern house blends in perfectly with the landscape and provides an insulated home.

The igloo house

This unique house has been designed, built, then buried, so that it blends into the surrounding landscape.

The man who designed it lives in Ontario, Canada, where the winters are freezing cold. He tried to keep the cold wind out of his cottage in winter and the warmth in using insulation, but his cottage was still freezing.

One winter, he built an igloo using thick snow blocks. He was surprised by how warm it was. The heat that came from people's bodies when they were inside the igloo was trapped by the thick snow blocks.

He decided to design a home using the same shape as an igloo. Although it was expensive to build, a lot of money will be saved over time on heating the house.

The igloo house was built under the ground.

skylights

windows

entrance

Conclusion

Today, some people still choose to live in underground homes for many good reasons.

Underground homes are insulated from both hot and cold conditions. This means that less energy is used to heat and cool homes. This is good for the environment. Living underground protects people from wild weather such as storms. Many underground homes blend in naturally with their environment and there is more room for gardens. In the future, even more people may choose to live under the ground.

Index

A note from the author

This was a difficult book to write,
but only because it was so interesting
that it was hard to know when to stop!
There were so many examples of
underground houses around the world,
and so much fascinating information,
that I just wanted to keep writing.

When researching underground homes,
I began an amazing and informative
journey that covered history, archaeology,
architecture and the environment.
It was like visiting a whole world of
underground living, and after a while
I began to think that it would be a
good idea if we all lived underground!